RAILWAY HISTORY IN PICTURES

Chilterns and Cotswolds

R. DAVIES and M.D.GRANT

DAVID & CHARLES
NEWTON ABBOT LONDON NORTH POMFRET (VT) VANCOUVER

'And then so many of the lines went such wonderful ways,
so crossing and curving among one another, that the eye lost them.'

Mugby Junction   Charles Dickens

ISBN 0 7153 7299 8
Library of Congress Catalog Card Number 76-58791

Photoset in 10 on 11 Times
printed and bound in Great Britain
by Redwood Burn Limited
for David & Charles (Publishers) Limited
Brunel House   Newton Abbot   Devon

Published in the United States of America
by David & Charles Inc
North Pomfret   Vermont 05053   USA

Published in Canada
by Douglas David & Charles Limited
1875 Welch Street   North Vancouver   BC

Contents

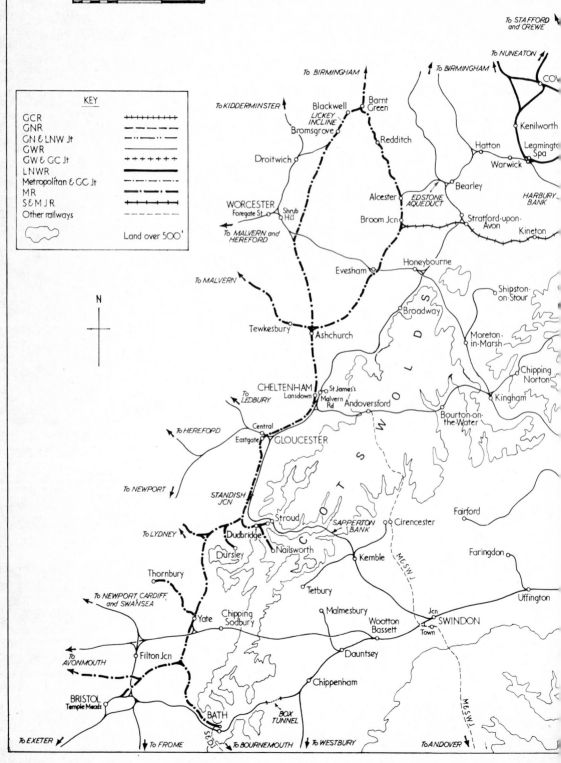

RAILWAYS IN THE CHILTERNS
AND COTSWOLDS

0   5   10   15 miles

KEY

GCR	+++++++
GNR	— — —
GN & LNW Jt	— · · — · · —
GWR	——————
GW & GC Jt	+—+—+—+
LNWR	▬▬▬▬
Metropolitan & GC Jt	— ▬ — ▬ —
M R	+—+—+—+
S & M J R	+++++
Other railways	— — — —

Land over 500'

N

To STAFFORD
and CREWE

To NUNEATON

To BIRMINGHAM

To BIRMINGHAM

COV

To KIDDERMINSTER
Blackwell
Barnt Green
LICKEY INCLINE
Bromsgrove
Droitwich
Redditch
Kenilworth
Hatton
Leamington Spa
Warwick
Bearley
Alcester
EDSTONE AQUEDUCT
HARBURY BANK
WORCESTER
Foregate St
Shrub Hill
Broom Jcn
Stratford-upon-Avon
Kineton
To MALVERN and HEREFORD
Evesham
Honeybourne
To MALVERN
Shipston-on-Stour
Broadway
Moreton-in-Marsh
Tewkesbury
Ashchurch
Chipping Norton
CHELTENHAM
St James's
Lansdown
Malvern Rd
Andoversford
Kingham
To LEDBURY
Central
Bourton-on-the-Water
To HEREFORD
Eastgate
GLOUCESTER
To NEWPORT
Fairford
STANDISH JCN
Stroud
SAPPERTON BANK
Cirencester
To LYDNEY
Dudbridge
Nailsworth
Kemble
Faringdon
Dursley
Uffington
Thornbury
Tetbury
To NEWPORT CARDIFF
and SWANSEA
Yate
Chipping Sodbury
Malmesbury
Wootton Bassett
SWINDON
Town
Jcn
Dauntsey
To AVONMOUTH
Filton Jcn
Chippenham
BRISTOL
Temple Meads
BATH
BOX TUNNEL
To EXETER
To FROME
To BOURNEMOUTH
To WESTBURY
To ANDOVER

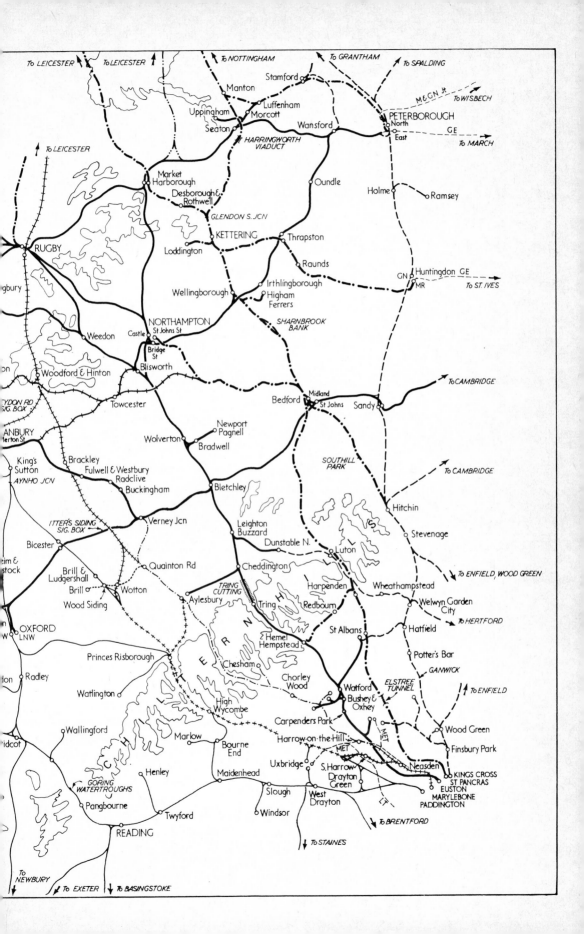

Frontispiece: A picture which sums up in one train the past and present, for it depicts what could have been a Great Western working of years past with GW Manor and Hall class mixed traffic 4-6-0s at the head of spotless GWR coaches. Yet the years are spanned for this is a 1974 shot of preserved locomotives Nos 7808 and 6998 from the GW Society depot at Didcot working a special train from Didcot to Stratford-upon-Avon near Kings Sutton.

J. G. Mallinson

Introduction

From London through Birmingham to Yorkshire and the North-West stretches the economic heartland of Britain, the source of industrial prosperity and the key to economic success. Yet in this heartland there are remnants of an older landscape and society, rooted in a rural past and redolent still of rural calm and charm. One such area is the real focus of this book, its boundaries lying between the metropolitan bustle of London and the industrial concentrations of Birmingham and the Black Country. It lacks an obvious name, but it has no shortage of character and cohesion with its largely unspoilt Cotswold villages and Chiltern scarplands which gradually merge with the undulating ridges and vales of the South Midlands to their north and east.

Its interest to the lover of railways stems from these two facets of its character. It is threaded by main lines linking London to the Midlands and North, lines alien to the area in one sense, but in their urgent striding across scarp and vale emphasising its role as a major corridor of movement. Other lines are inherent to the area itself, their rural charm an effective counterpoint to main line majesty. Many of these country byways are now but memories, for they were early victims of the waves of railway closures. Their story has already been told in *Forgotten Railways: Chilterns & Cotswolds* but in this pictorial volume their memory is revived.

This book seeks to portray the visual impact of the railway on this varied area. With five major, three minor and two joint lines in pre-grouping days, there was no shortage of variety. Grouping replaced seven of the ten by three main line companies while nationalisation in turn brought three regions. However, in spite of its latent geographical interest and constituent railway company development, it seemed right that treatment should be by theme to provide the flavour of the area and to compare and contrast the railways which served it.

Any introduction would be incomplete without a special thanks to all those who have helped with this volume whom, owing to lack of space, we are unable to name individually.

R.D. and M.D.G.

1 Railways in the Scene

By 1837, railways were certainly not new, for this was some years after the pioneer Stockton & Darlington and Liverpool & Manchester Railways had led the way. However, 1838 was to see the start of a new era – the 'main line' had arrived in the form of the London & Birmingham Railway, which in later years under LNW rule was to be known as the 'Premier Line'.

Although first, in 1837, to pierce the Chiltern hills separating the capital and Home Counties from the Midlands, other competitors were following close behind. Hotly pursuing was the Great Western, the first stage of its London to Bristol main line of which was opened in 1838, forming the southern boundary of the area. These two companies, together with the LNW's grouping partner of 1923, the Midland, vied bitterly to develop a considerable part of the railway network of the area.

The year 1850 heralded the opening of the Great Northern along the eastern perimeter of the area which, with the London extension of the Great Central, was destined at grouping to bring the newly formed LNER into the heart of the territory.

The railway manias of the mid-19th century stimulated the construction of branch and secondary routes which reached into the hinterland by-passed by the main lines. The peace of these rural counties was to remain largely undisturbed, for many of the branches never became more than purely local amenities serving the scattered villages and market townships and their attendant agricultural industries predominant in the area.

In setting the scene it is difficult in just a few photographs to express more than the essential nature of the railways of the Chilterns and Cotswolds. More detailed aspects of the railway scene in the region are explored in the succeeding chapters.

Above The complete transformation of the railway industry over the years is clear from this everyday scene at Cheddington in 1914. Even at that time, when road transport was mainly horse-drawn, the benefits of the motor lorry were realised and it was soon used to the detriment of the railway.   *F. Goodwin Collection*

Left Watford has been a junction since 1858 when the LNW's St Albans branch was opened. Until then its original station, shown in this early portrait, was to the north of the St Albans Road bridge. The station increased in importance in 1862 with the opening of the Rickmansworth branch and still further on becoming the northern terminus of the electrified 'New Line', the LNW's local suburban service, and the Croxley Green branch in the second decade of this century. Although its importance as a junction has waned, it has since become a key railhead on the LMR electrified main line.
G. Cornwall Collection

Above: As a storm approaches the Chilterns, the level crossing gates are closed at Fulwell & Westbury for a train from Verney Junction to Banbury (Merton Street). This line was built with the aim of uniting Buckinghamshire by railways in the form of a cross intersecting at Verney Junction. In the event, only the Oxford to Bletchley and Verney Junction to Banbury sections of the Buckinghamshire Railway were completed as planned.
Alan J. Willmott

Right: The junction signalbox was once a commonplace part of the railway scene, now rapidly disappearing. Broom North box controlled local movements on the Midland's Barnt Green to Ashchurch loop line and SMJ services to and from Stratford and beyond.
John Horne

Above: Rural branches somehow possessed a timelessness which has been lost forever. Typical of many similar examples throughout the country, the Midland branch from Hemel Hempsted (using the spelling then current on the railway) to Harpenden never seemed to date. Redbourn, seen in 1920, was closed to passengers in 1947 but part of the line still carries freight under private ownership. *H. J. Patterson Rutherford*

Below: Sometimes a junction was more important for exchange of traffic than for the locality it served. Seaton, junction of the Peterborough, Rugby and Stamford lines and terminus for the Uppingham branch, was such a case. A train from Peterborough draws into the platform while the Uppingham branch train waits in the bay. *Rev A. W. V. Mace*

2 Main Lines

The area covered by this book was crossed by main lines of rather more than average historical note. It possessed one of the first and last trunk lines to be built and the first major main line to be closed. While the trunk lines radiating from London had their objectives further afield, the main line companies spread their influence throughout the area by secondary and branch routes, often planned with strategic inter-company rivalry in mind. Thus the Great Western tried strenuously to force the broad gauge into the heart of LNW territory in the Midlands. Similarly the Midland, and later the Great Central, came south from their Midland domains to London through established LNW and GN country.

The backbone of the railway network in the Chilterns and Cotswolds was largely planned by the mid-19th century. Yet considerable development continued, culminating in the opening of the London extension of the Great Central in 1899, followed in 1906 by the completion of the Great Western & Great Central Joint line from Ashendon via High Wycombe and Beaconsfield to Northolt Junction.

Many famous named trains such as the *Coronation Scot*, the *Flying Scotsman* or the *Bristolian* brought interest to main lines of the area while summer Saturdays produced added variety on holiday trains from the North to the South and West. Motive power of every kind could be seen over the years from 'Bloomers' to Scots, ancient broad gauge veterans to Kings, Stirling singles to A3s, while record breaking *Mallard* could be seen regularly striding through the Northern Heights at Hadley Wood.

Today the main line scene is ceaselessly changing. On the one hand the Great Central is now no more than a memory. On the other, the many acres of marshalling yards essential to the movement of wagonload goods trains have been largely replaced by the freightliner depot. Regular inter-city services, electrically worked on the main line from Euston, and diesel elsewhere, now make the once proud named steam era expresses appear like semi-fast services as the main lines are prepared for the HST and APT. Such changes only serve to enhance the nostalgia of the main lines of yesteryear.

Below: On the southern fringes of the Cotswolds, King Class 4-6-0 No 6015 *King Richard III* takes the down *Merchant Venturer* unobtrusively past Sydney Gardens on the outskirts of the gracious city of Bath. *D. H. Ballantyne*

Top left: To obtain a foothold in the West, the Midland snapped up the Birmingham & Gloucester and Bristol & Gloucester railways in 1846 giving it direct access into GW territory. Ashchurch, at the southern extremity of the Vale of Evesham, subsequently became a junction for Midland branches to Evesham and Tewkesbury. Here, compound 4-4-0 No 41047 enters Ashchurch on a southbound local in September 1949. The flat crossing linking the two branches at right angles to the main line can be seen behind the engine. *H. C. Casserley*

Above: Straddling the Cotswolds and the Vale of Evesham, the Oxford, Worcester & Wolverhampton Railway passed through some delightful countryside on its way to the Black Country. The OW&W station in Evesham was opened in 1852 and shared a common station approach road with the Midland, whose services from Ashchurch commenced in 1864. Modified Hall class 4-6-0 No 7911 *Lady Margaret Hall* restarts a Moreton-in-Marsh to Worcester (Shrub Hill) local from Evesham in April 1962. *M. Mensing*

Left: Before the opening of the Severn Tunnel in December 1886, GW trains for South Wales had to travel via Gloucester. The tunnel shortened the route from Paddington by 15 miles and since 1903 the majority of South Wales trains have used the line via Badminton. Modified Hall class 4-6-0 No 7909 *Heveningham Hall* emerges from Sodbury Tunnel on to the watertroughs with a down freight on 15 June 1962. *Colin G. Maggs*

Below: A major railway opening must have been an exciting affair, with its display of bunting, the enthusiastic support of the town band, the inevitable feasting by those involved in the promotion of the line and the public holiday usually granted in the locality. The scene at Brackley Central on Thursday 9 March 1899, witnessed by many local dignitaries, was no exception. Yet it is difficult to envisage the reaction of the crowd had they known that another mournful group would be witnessing the last train on the London Extension of the Great Central only 67 years later. Closure, by contrast, was sad and ignominious, an unfitting end to such a noble beginning.
Northamptonshire Record Office Ref. YZ 4191

Right: Inter-regional cross-country services were a feature of the area. Ex GN 4-4-2 Atlantic No 3299 marshals the stock of an inter-company service from Sheffield, bound for South Wales at Oxford during lunchtime on 25 October 1936. The same LNER locomotive generally worked through from Leicester to Swindon, travelling over foreign metals south of Banbury.
Rev A. W. V. Mace

Bottom right: Hall class 4-6-0 No 5981 *Frensham Hall* hurries a York to Bournemouth express through Aynho in the late 1950s. Such trains, which took several routes from north to south across the area, were heavily used on summer Saturdays by holidaymakers from the North of England visiting South Coast resorts.
Real Photographs Co Ltd Ref T8967

Right: Anglo-Scottish rivals, the LNW and the GN both afforded good opportunities to watch main line steam in action. Carpenders Park, in August 1919, provides an interesting combination of steam at speed, together with the original station and open countryside which no longer exist. The wooden platforms serving the 'New Line' were replaced in 1952 by a central island platform to serve the large housing estates that had been built up on both sides of the line.

H. J. Patterson Rutherford

Bottom right: Hatfield, too, has changed considerably since this photograph of Class A1 4-6-2 No 60117 *Bois Roussel* was taken in April 1959. Its train, the up Yorkshire Pullman, is an example of a number of Pullman services which at one time could be seen on the main lines of the area and which culminated in the dieselised Blue Pullmans of the Midland and Western Region routes, and the electrically-hauled Pullmans of the West Coast route. *Ron Wood*

Below Above: In June 1957, Stanier Class 5 4-6-0 No 44848 draws a northbound express out of Wellingborough, an interesting junction station at the crossroads of the South Midlands. Behind the down slow platform the bay used by Higham Ferrers branch trains can be seen, while a spur to the LNW Northampton to Peterborough line curved off to the right just to the south of the station. *Chris Cheetham Collection*

3 Cross-Country Services

Cross-country lines which augmented the railway network were an intermediate stage between main lines and branches. Trains on these lines were generally semi-fast or stopping services which provided a haven for locomotives and coaches which had retired from the strain of regular main line work. They were normally formed of three or four coaches hauled by tender engines or tanks with a push-pull set.

These lines developed in a number of different ways. Usually they were promoted by an independent company which sold out to one of the major railways soon after the line was opened. Some, however, like the Midland & South Western Junction or the Stratford-upon-Avon & Midland Junction continued their independent existence until grouping in 1923. More typically, the Banbury & Cheltenham Direct sold out to the Great Western in 1897, 10 years after the line was finally opened throughout; the Kettering,

Thrapstone & Huntingdon, worked by the Midland from the outset, was absorbed by it in 1897 and the LNW Oxford to Cambridge route comprised railways constructed by three separate companies. By contrast the London & Birmingham was instrumental in the promotion of branches from its main line to Luffenham, Peterborough, and Dunstable which in the last case, by connection with a Great Northern branch, provided a through route to Hatfield. The Great Western's Birmingham to Cheltenham route was undertaken in the 1900s as a part of a programme of works to give shorter distances between its main centres.

Whatever their derivation, these lines enabled travellers to avoid detours via main towns, and cross-country expresses could make use of a plethora of different routes that nowadays they are denied.

Below: To provide an alternative route to the Midland Railway between Birmingham and Cheltenham, the Great Western opened new lines from Tyseley to Bearley to passengers in 1908 and from Honeybourne to Cheltenham in stages from 1904 to 1906, doubling the existing branch between Bearley and Honeybourne.

Despite the sparse population, stopping services were provided, and 0-4-2T No 1424, with the 13.17 Honeybourne to Cheltenham, calls briefly at Hayles Abbey Halt in 1960, cascading water from an over-full tank.
D. H. Ballantyne

Right: The Rugby to Stamford route opened throughout in 1851 but to provide the LNW with a more direct link from Peterborough to Birmingham, a new line was opened between Seaton and Wansford in 1879. This left a shuttle between Seaton and Stamford and the section to the junction with the Midland at Luffenham was reduced to single line in 1880. BR Standard 2-6-2T No 84008 emerges from Morcott Tunnel with a Stamford train in 1964.
P. H. Wells

Right: Stratford-upon-Avon was the headquarters of the combined system and its principal locomotive depot. To the left the lines led round to a junction with the Great Western and to the right onwards to Broom, where it joined the Midland. The presence of many Midland 0-6-0s indicates the influence of the LMS and on the extreme right are the turntable and coaling stage.
Locomotive & General Railway Photographs

Bottom right: Closure came piecemeal, with the section from Olney to Towcester closing to passengers as early as March 1893, four months after opening. Passenger services on the portion of the Northampton & Banbury Junction, one of its constituents, between Cockley Brake Junction and Towcester were withdrawn on 2 July 1951; 44204 stands at Banbury (Merton Street) with the last train, a sight that was to become increasingly familiar throughout the area in the next 20 years.
Locomotive & General Railway Photographs

Below: The Stratford-upon-Avon & Midland Junction Railway was an idiosyncratic merger of four companies whose services extended from Olney in the east to Broom in the west. Both the amalgamated company and its constituents led a penurious existence and were merged into the LMS in 1923.

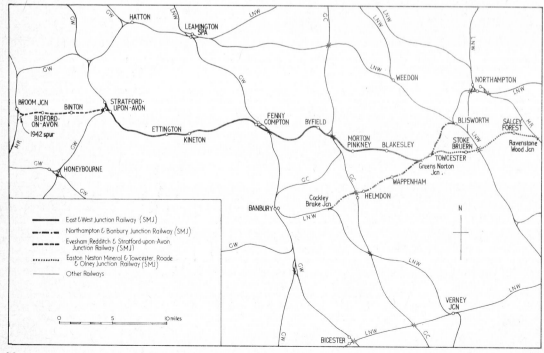

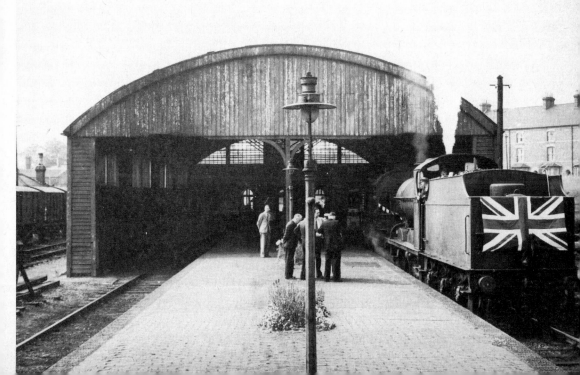

Above: Having extended the Bourton-on-the-Water and Chipping Norton branches to Cheltenham and Kings Sutton respectively, the Banbury & Cheltenham Direct Railway opened throughout in 1887 but until 1906 no direct connection existed at Kingham between its two sections. Even then services remained distinct and in 1962 No 5184 on the 10.50 Cheltenham St James to Kingham train meets sister engine No 4101 with the 11.18 from Kingham at Bourton-on-the-Water.

D. H. Ballantyne

Below: Running from Red Post Junction near Andover to Andoversford, the Midland & South Western Junction Railway provided a through service between Southampton and Cheltenham but was only intensively used in the two World Wars. By 1936 it had become just another part of the Great Western and its Swindon offices on the right, closed in 1924, looked out at No 3285 *Katerfelto* on a Cheltenham to Southampton train.

Rev A. W. V. Mace

Above: Webb 0-6-2T No 58887 is about to depart from Leighton Buzzard for Dunstable North, where the LNW made an end-on junction with the GN branch from Hatfield. Originally the LNW branch was intended to terminate at Luton but determined opposition delayed Luton's railway until 1858 and the LNW never really gained a foothold in Luton, despite the running powers it was granted over the GN to Bute Street.   *W. T. Baldwin*

Below: An early branch of the London & Birmingham was the Northampton & Peterborough Railway, a long tentacle to the Eastern Counties Railway. Originally it was single track from Northampton to Peterborough with a crossing place at Thrapston. Trains were timed to meet there so locomotives, which were confined to their respective sections, could be exchanged. Much later, Class 5 4-6-0 No 45292 with a Northampton to Peterborough train runs into Irthlingborough.

Ian L. Wright

Above: Although within the LMR, the Kettering to Huntingdon line saw former GE engines in BR days on Kettering to Cambridge trains, exemplified by Class J 15 0-6-0 No 65475 at Raunds with a Kettering train in 1957.

Ian L. Wright

Left: As part of a programme of estate improvements, Captain William Peel opened a private railway from the Great Northern at Sandy to Potton in 1857. Although successful, it was incorporated into the Bedford & Cambridge Railway, opened in 1862 and absorbed into the LNW in 1865. Sandy thus became an intermediate station on the Oxford to Cambridge line as well as a GN station, staffed until 1917 by both companies.

M. Mensing

4 Rural Byways

Having established the basic network of main line and secondary routes through the area, the gaps missed by the primary lines were in most cases filled by branch lines serving mainly rural localities. Many small country townships on the main lines thus achieved minor importance as railway junctions when branch lines were opened, examples including Kemble, Kingham, Alcester, Hatfield and Seaton.

The majority of these rural byways now no longer exist, having succumbed to the economic pressures of the latter half of the 20th century. A good proportion of these antiquities, however, did survive until comparatively recently and the photographs included will revive memories of far off summer days spent in the country.

The scene shows 0-6-0PT No 1658 waiting at Kemble on a Tetbury branch local before dieselisation of the branch in 1959. Situated almost midway between Swindon and Gloucester near the source of the Thames, Kemble was also junction for Cirencester where the line from Swindon originally terminated before completion in 1845 of the through facility from Kemble to Standish Junction and Gloucester. *R. E. Toop*

How many of the lines could have ever justified construction is debatable, but they were often promoted with the greatest optimism. Nor, indeed, did many of them die without a struggle, although it is sad to think that had more of the group witnessing the last train supported services at other times, facilities may just have survived. Unfortunately, the day of the branch line belonged to another age before cars, lorries and the motor bus.

Yet in spite of the Beeching closure programme, some comparatively unimportant byways miraculously survive so that it is still possible to sample something of this atmosphere. Services such as Watford to St Albans, Princes Risborough to Aylesbury, Bletchley to Bedford, Maidenhead to Marlow and Redditch to Barnt Green still maintain the rural flavour and operation with which they were founded. Dying, but not yet dead, they remain memorials to the once common branch line.

Above: On the final day of operation in 1962 on the Redditch to Evesham section of the Midland loop line, through the Vale of Evesham, Class 2 2-6-0 No 46492 is seen leaving Redditch on the 13.12 Birmingham (New Street) to Evesham train. Passenger facilities south of Evesham lingered until June 1963 but the section from Barnt Green to Redditch has been retained as part of the Birmingham commuter network. *M. Mensing*

Top right: In the heart of ex GW territory in the Cotswolds 0-6-0PT 8743 waits with the Kingham train at Chipping Norton on 29 July 1960. This section, opened in 1855, was eventually to become part of a useful cross-country link across the Cotswolds between Banbury and Cheltenham. Passenger services east of Chipping Norton, which had been introduced in 1887, were withdrawn from 4 June 1951 although facilities to Kingham continued until 3 December 1962. *Rae Montgomery*

Right: In the Chiltern Foothills branches from Hatfield and Leighton Buzzard to Dunstable also provided useful east to west cross-country links. Some of the finest Hertfordshire countryside was between Harpenden and Ayot on the ex GN branch, beautifully illustrated by Wheathampstead station shrouded by woodland. Passenger services were withdrawn from 26 April 1965. *Alan J. Willmott*

On the edge of the Chilterns in rural North Buckinghamshire, photographer *H. C. Casserley* masterfully captures the idyllic summertime mood of many former rural byways.

Radclive (*above*) and Water Stratford Halts near Buckingham were opened in 1956 concurrently with an imaginative dieselisation experiment aimed to attract traffic and save railway services from Bletchley to Banbury (Merton Street). As the advertising board shows, every effort was made to stimulate longer distance off-peak travel from this remote country hamlet which was served by trains for less than five years.

Through the woods just south of Brill & Ludgershall station on the former GW Birmingham direct main line (*top right*), 0-6-0PT No 5419 quietly passes with a Banbury to Princes Risborough motor train service in the heat of a June day in 1935. Such trains, which called at all the rural wayside stations, were typical of services provided in sparsely populated country areas before the full impact of more flexible motor bus competition resulted in their withdrawal.

Within yards of the previous scene, Metropolitan Class A 4-4-0T No 23 slips through the trees into Wood Siding station on the Brill branch (*right*), then operated by London Transport. Surviving remarkably into the 1930s as a haven of railway antiquity, it is not surprising that such a line, built to serve the Duke of Buckingham's private estates at Wotton, should have created so much interest.

Above: On many of the former LNW branches throughout the area after nationalisation, Ivatt Class 2 2-6-2Ts provided the staple motive power on passenger trains No 41227 draws quietly into Birdingbury station for the last time on the final train between Rugby and Leamington Spa (Milverton) on 13 June 1959.

M. Mensing

Top left: Verney Junction saw the expansion of the Metropolitan Railway halted in open fields in a remote part of North Buckinghamshire. The scene shows the station, which provided interchange with the Bletchley to Oxford and Buckingham services of the LNW, as it was in 1936 just before withdrawal of Met trains.

Sketch by Fraser Cameron

Left: Opened in 1867, the Wolverton to Newport Pagnell branch was partially constructed on the bed of the Newport Pagnell canal which diverged from the Grand Junction Canal at Great Linford. The trackbed of the closed branch in the vicinity of Bradwell is now in turn used as a footpath in the new city of Milton Keynes.

M. Mensing

Right: Sister engine No 41279 storms up the grade towards Uppingham on a branch train from Seaton on 12 March 1960. Opened to passengers on 1 October 1894, the branch maintained a close association with Uppingham School and towards the end of its life was operated by ex LT&S and GN 4-4-2 tanks.   *P. H. Wells*

33

5 Suburban Influences

Much of the south-eastern part of the area has been dominated since the mid-19th century by the influence of the Metropolis. The Chiltern hills, which in the embryonic years of railway development formed a physical barrier to the north and north-west of London, provided some problems to the main line companies wishing to develop the ever growing population of the inner suburbs, the need for suburban development overtook the disadvantages of the physical terrain leading eventually to the growth of commuter services into the Chilterns.

The railway commuter network, never really developed to the same extent as that south of the Thames, probably because of the extensive Underground railway system built throughout North London and of the unresponsiveness of the main line railway companies to the growing suburban market. Nevertheless, GN services into the Northern Heights and later Midland, LNW and GW local services did much to stimulate urban development along main lines.

Meriting special mention for its outstanding efforts to develop suburban traffic in the Chilterns, however, was the Metropolitan Railway which, throughout the 1920s and 1930s, capitalised on its 'Metro-land' brainchild, partially in league with the LNER. Met style houses were built first in the fields of Harrow, Pinner and Uxbridge, and later in the Chiltern towns of Chorley Wood, Chalfont, Chesham and Amersham.

Although no longer steam hauled, many of these facilities are still operated either by London Transport or as part of the BR suburban network. Dieselisation and electrification of the main lines have in recent years resulted in the expansion of the commuter area, with longer distance commuting from towns such as Reading, High Wycombe, Bletchley, Bedford and Hitchin. Such development was not found elsewhere in the area except at the northern and south-western extremities where the Birmingham and Bristol conurbations exerted some minor influence.

Right: The Metropolitan main line originally terminated at Chesham, deep in the Chilterns, but after the opening in 1892 of the extension from Chalfont to Aylesbury, the single track line to Chesham was reduced to a branch. Services were for some years operated by ex GC Class C13 4-4-2T tanks; No 67416 is seen leaving Chesham for Chalfont in the summer of 1955.
Alan J. Willmott

Left: Apart from the conversion of Metropolitan trains from steam to electric traction, the approaches to Harrow-on-the-Hill station in 1913 seem little different from today. *H. J. Patterson Rutherford*

Below: Reminiscent of similar motor train services in the nearby Chilterns, 0-4-2T No 1446 makes an attractive study at Drayton Green on the Ealing to Greenford shuttle. Steam was replaced by diesel units in 1958 which still provide the service. *Alan J. Willmott*

Left: The LNW and GC were comparative latecomers in the provision of inner suburban facilities, not introducing their services until the early 20th century. Through the once picturesque Middlesex countryside, the GC opened its own line between Neasden and Northolt to link with the GW&GC joint line from Ashendon Junction providing a second approach to its Marylebone terminus. On this line, GC 4-4-2T No 47 pauses at South Harrow station (today named Sudbury Hill, Harrow) in 1910.
British Rail Eastern Region

Bottom left: As part of its New Line electrification work in the Watford area, the LNW diverted the new local tracks, north of Bushey, west of the main line in a broad arc across the Colne Valley. The photograph shows a southbound inspection special crossing the Colne on the impressive brick viaduct on the opening day, 10 February 1913. Euston bound local services on the New Line remained steam hauled until 1922.
Radio Times Hulton Picture Library

Below: From its Broad Street terminus, by running powers over the GN and LNW, the North London Railway provided services into the Northern Heights, the remnants of which operated until 1976 when new GN line electric trains to Moorgate superseded them. Through country today retaining a pleasant rural air saved by the Green Belt, in earlier years North London 4-4-0T No 5 hurries past Ganwick signalbox between Potters Bar and Hadley Wood with a train of four wheel stock.
Locomotive Publishing Co by courtesy of Ian Allan Ltd

6 Passenger Services

Across Chiltern scarp and vale or between peaceful Cotswold villages, a wide variety of service was offered to the travelling public. In less busy days, with the aid of *Bradshaw*, connections to most places throughout the area could be found, often with a journey at one end on a quiet rural branch line with its own particular charm and brand of operation. It was not uncommon to leave the noise and bustle of Euston or Paddington by a morning train to be met after lunch at the most peaceful of country stations, although for some journeys the multiplicity of services meant a decision on the best route to take.

Buses and taxis replaced horse flys and gigs in the station forecourts but now the country station has closed, necessitating a car trip to the nearest railhead. Polite porters, pushing barrows or trolleys, would help ladies from the carriages and heave heavy trunks from the guards van at the start of the long summer holiday in the country. Wooden steps from the platform were a common feature at the wayside stations and halts throughout the area.

Until the conversion to electric light at the principal stations, flickering gas and oil lamps lit the path of the night traveller, while foot-warmers were often given to rural branch passengers on cold winter evenings! Race specials came to Towcester, Stratford and Cheltenham, while school specials made connections with services to all parts of the country at the beginning and end of terms. The companies always did their best to encourage travel, with excursion tickets to London or days out in the countryside.

Although often inconvenient for the villages they purported to serve, the rural branch could sometimes be a lifeline in the depths of winter for somehow the train could usually get through. Yet these, like the billowing steam from the passing express, have now gone forever.

Above: Tank engines at work; the branch train from Harpenden stands at Hemel Hempsted in 1920. The Midland branch continued to a passenger terminus at Heath Park Halt, although goods were taken into the LNW yard at Boxmoor. *H. J. Patterson Rutherford*

Left: Coasting through a speed restricted section for track relaying in the Chilterns, Class B 17 4-6-0 No 2842 *Kilverstone Hall* passes Chorley Wood with a Marylebone–Sheffield express on 2 June 1934. *H. C. Casserley*

Below: Under leaden skies, GW 0-6-0PT No 8743 braves a cold January day at Evesham during the hard winter of 1963. The truncated passenger services south of Evesham, which were operated by WR locomotives after closure of the section from Redditch, were withdrawn from 17 June 1963. *E. Wilmshurst*

39

Above: Class 4F 0-6-0 No 44188 takes one of the last passenger workings, an enthusiasts' special over the SMJ between Ettington and Kineton on 24 April 1965. Towards the end of steam, the area saw its fair share of steam hauled specials which often brought unusual locomotive workings.   *T. Stephens*

Top right: An interesting but not unique facility seen in the area were slip coaches. To provide certain intermediate stations with a fast service without stopping expresses, coaches were slipped from selected trains. In August 1960, Hall class 4-6-0 No 5994 *Roydon Hall* picks up the slip coach at Bicester off the 17.10 Paddington to Wolverhampton express which it will take on the front of its own train, the 16.34 Paddington to Wolverhampton semi-fast.   *M. Mensing*

Right: Near Calvert, Prince of Wales class 4-6-0 No 25845 has just passed beneath the GC main line at Itters Sidings signalbox with an Oxford bound passenger train on 13 May 1939.   *H. C. Casserley*

7 Freight Facilities

Although passenger trains captured the attention, it was freight that provided the initial stimulus for railways. Individual unbraked wagons, many privately owned, were the units upon which the system was based. Each station had a goods yard, in contrast to the small number of mechanised depots today, while private sidings served local industry. Linking these was the pick-up freight, taking wagons to the nearest marshalling yard to be formed into trains for trunk haul. Each wagon might pass through several yards until it reached one where it would be attached to another local freight for delivery.

With many individual companies in pregrouping days, revenue for freight and parcels had to be apportioned between the companies. To settle inter-company indebtedness the Railway Clearing House was established in 1842, and in 1847 it was agreed 'That the wagon tellers . . . at . . . Rugby, Northampton etc be placed under . . . the Clearing House'. Established some years earlier, number takers were employed at junctions to report the movements of wagons, carriages and tarpaulins.

The Clearing House *Handbook of Stations* included details of facilities for *inter alia* cattle and horses, neither of which are now carried by train. Further freight flows which have ceased are coal bound for London on the Midland, bananas from Avonmouth on the SMJ, Grimsby fish on the GN, hats from Luton, fruit from the Vale of Evesham and iron ore from Oxfordshire. Today freight runs increasingly in trainloads and not always by the most obvious direct route, for freight routes have been rationalised to make best use of diminished facilities or to keep slower freights out of the way of high speed inter-city passenger trains.

To cater for considerable flows of ironstone traffic from Oxfordshire to South Wales, new junctions were laid at Fenny Compton and Stratford-upon-Avon (*below*). Opened in 1960, they enabled the SMJ to be used to avoid Hatton bank on the GW main line. 2-6-2T No 4176 (*bottom*), on an iron ore train from Ardley, comes off the down Bicester line at Aynho in 1962, having crossed the Oxford lines on the flyover.

M. Mensing

Below left: Ten of the BR Standard Class 9F 2-10-0 locomotives were equipped with Crosti double-barrelled boilers as an experiment when introduced in 1955. They were based at Wellingborough and found their principal use on freight trains from the East Midlands to London. No 92024, one of these locomotives, all of which subsequently had the experimental preheater boiler removed, takes the line towards Roade on restarting from Northampton Castle with an up freight in 1961.

M. Mensing

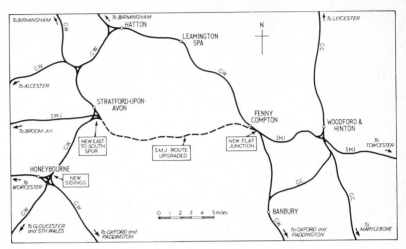

Above: With such large fleets of wagons, maintenance was essential and at Worcester the Great Western owned considerable shops to repair wagon sheets, stacks of which can be seen in the centre of the picture. To the left can be seen the shops of Wagon Repairs Ltd, a private company unconnected with the railway, which specialised in the repair of wagons and which is still operating today.

British Rail, Western Region

Top right: As an off-shoot from its main Bristol to Birmingham line, the Midland owned a branch from Stonehouse which bifurcated at Dudbridge for Stroud and Nailsworth. Class 3F 0-6-0 No 43373, with a pick-up goods of eight wagons, typical of those trains which meandered along attaching and detaching wagons, passes Dudbridge Junction signal box en route to Nailsworth in 1955.

D. H. Ballantyne

Right: The 'Vinegar Works Line' in Worcester, privately owned but maintained and operated by the GW, was 900 yards long and served the sidings of Hill Evans & Co. Opened in 1872, trains were restricted to 4mph over the road crossings, where road traffic was controlled by railway lower quadrant signals. Gradients limited the maximum number of wagons to 12 and a return trip took 45 min.

Rev A. W. V. Mace

Above: Any large centre would have shunting locomotives busy in the goods yards and sidings. Typical of such scenes is D2909 at work in the yard at the west end of Rugby Midland station in 1961. In the background is the main covered goods shed, while a mobile crane is available to unload wagons out in the yard, and cattle wagons stand beside the cattle dock. *M. Mensing*

Below: Dunstable North exemplifies the small goods yard. In this once commonplace scene, coal merchants are filling sacks from the wagons, two vans stand in the platform ready for parcels traffic while others are being unloaded in the goods shed. A loading gauge stands on the approaches, points in the yard are hand operated, shunt signals abound, a gas lamp acts as illumination and there are still wooden-bodied wagons. *Brian Parnell*

8 Railway Centres

Throughout the railway network, lines became concentrated at a number of centres where the routes of one or perhaps more companies met. Sometimes, as in the case of Northampton, they were existing towns which different companies were anxious to serve. Elsewhere, as at Seaton in the Welland Valley, physical geography dictated that lines of communication should meet. While the railway added an impetus to growth in existing settlements, in some instances it was responsible for the growth of villages into railway towns. In these places, Swindon, Wolverton and Woodford Halse, for example, the railway had to build housing, provide services and generally exercise a paternal sway over the community.

Peterborough was one centre where both influences were at work. Formerly a sleepy cathedral and market town, the coming of the railway, particularly the extensive New England estate provided by the Great Northern, saw its population and influence grow in the 21 years it took to build up its railway network. Both passenger stations, North and East, were hamstrung until 1913 and 1934 respectively by immediately adjacent level crossings, while North suffered from a 20 mph speed restriction on the curved approach to its southern end. Improvements to North station were mooted as early as 1898 but finally reached fruition in 1973.

Peterborough points to a general rule. Irrespective of their derivation railway centres developed to no overall plan although the passage of time diluted the influence of the railway, and in many cases the complex layouts with duplicate facilities were not rationalised until after nationalisation.

Below: Bletchley was one of the LNW barn stations, large overall roofs of glass and steel which the signals had to overcome by great height. Situated where the Oxford to Cambridge service crossed the main line on the level, it boasted a motive power depot and marshalling yards, although the station was considerably rebuilt at the time of electrification, including what became a very expensive and later virtually redundant flyover. *H. C. Casserley*

Above: At Huntingdon the Great Northern main line met the Midland from Kettering and the Great Northern & Great Eastern joint line from St Ives. In this December 1910 view, taken from Huntingdon East, the Kettering line crosses the river bridge behind the GN signalbox, and joins the Joint line curving away to the left. East station, opened in 1883, was designed by the Great Northern, whose station lies to the right.

British Rail, Eastern Region

Below: Peterborough was served by three stations and five railways of which three are represented in a 1938 view of the south end of the Great Northern station. No 4518 on the left is a former Great Northern locomotive, while No 083 is from the Midland & Great Northern Joint. On the extreme left is Crescent Sidings signalbox controlling the Midland lines, which had their own station at Crescent until 1866. *H. C. Casserley*

Above: An epitome of the railway age is the LNW station in Oxford in 1914, which was graced by a circular booking office purchased from the 1851 Exhibition. Despite the immaculate condition of its staff and equipment, the LNW was overshadowed by the GW, whose numerous routes radiated from its adjacent station. As befitted its cosmopolitan nature, locomotives of all four grouping companies could be seen at Oxford.

Oxfordshire County Libraries

Below: BR Class 2 2-6-2T No 84005 leaves Bedford in March 1958 with a stopping train to Hitchin that will follow the Midland's original approach to London, crossing the LNW line to Bletchley en route by a flat crossing. The St Pancras extension of 1868 left the original line at Bedford Junction, and the Midland Station was altered, leaving a complex layout, slightly eased by an avoiding line for expresses opened in 1894.

T. E. Rounthwaite

Above: In some cases the complex nature of the railway network can only be fully appreciated from the air. Rugby centres on the LNW station in the middle of the photograph with the Midland from Leicester (*top right*) the Leamington, Coventry and LNW main line (*top*) and the Peterborough (*bottom centre*) and London and Northampton lines (*bottom left*) focussing on it. Just below the station, the Great Central crosses the LNW from right to left on its course southwards towards London.

Aerofilms Limited

Right: Arrangements at Gloucester have always been complex and defy neat solutions. Scene of the break of gauge controversy between 4ft $8\frac{1}{2}$in and 7ft $0\frac{1}{4}$in, it was served by the Midland and the Great Western which left a legacy of level crossings and duplicate facilities. The two stations, Great Western at the top centre of the photograph and Midland top right, were linked by a 250 yd long footbridge along which generations of weary passengers have trudged.

Aerofilms Limited

51

The three railway towns of the area were Swindon, Wolverton and Woodford Halse.

Selected by Brunel and Gooch as the principal locomotive works of the Great Western, Swindon (*right*) was a locomotive change-over point and the meeting of the main line and the Cheltenham branch, worked by the GW. Opened in 1843 with 300 workmen, expansion and the transfer of the carriage workshops from Paddington saw a population of 1,580 in 1821 grow to 19,904 in 1881, approximately the date of this view of the west end. Mixed gauge is apparent on the Bristol line, leading off to the left of the works, and on the Gloucester branch. The locomotive works lies in the angle made by the two lines, while the locomotive shed lies to the right beyond the GW Medical Fund Swimming Bath. Notice the complicated trackwork caused by swinging the standard gauge rails from one side to the other of the broad gauge lines.
Wiltshire Library and Museum Service Swindon Divisional Library

Wolverton Works was originally opened by the London & Birmingham Railway at the halfway point on its system. Changes in LNW policy after 1860 concentrated locomotive construction at Crewe and left Wolverton to specialise in carriage and wagon engineering. Expansion of the railway estate was hampered after 1850 by the principal local landowner who would not sell sufficient land to meet LNW requirements. A population of 417 in 1831 grew to 3,611 in 1881 but diversification began with McCorquodale's printing works in 1878. Development spread down the main Stratford road along which the 3ft 6in gauge Wolverton & Stony Stratford Tramway opened in 1887. About 700 workmen were carried daily by its services, one of which is shown (*bottom right*) outside the main entrance to the works circa 1913.
Wolverton and District Archaeological Society

Woodford Halse owed its development to the Great Central Railway which established yards and a locomotive depot to service its London extension (*map, below right*). The decade between 1891 and 1901 saw the population grow from 527 to 1,220 and to 1,520 by 1911. Goods services were run principally either via Banbury or the Stratford-upon-Avon & Midland Junction and the railway brought considerable employment. Yet the dependence on the railway meant that the closure of the depot and yards in 1965 was a serious blow to the town.

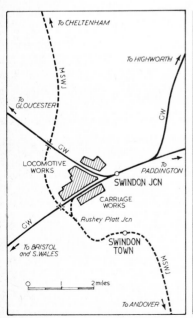

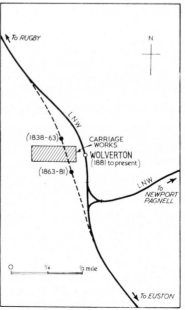

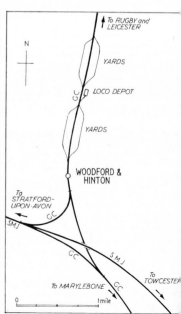

9 Inclines and Gradients

With potentially difficult terrain to cross, like the canals, railways through the area could either follow the contours, tunnel, or if a cheap, direct route was needed, climb the hills. Possibly the finest engineered stretch of line in the area was the Great Central north of Quainton Road where, because of its relatively modern construction and for the benefit of speed, gradients were made as easy as possible by embankments, cuttings, viaducts and tunnels. Such construction was, however, very expensive and many of the older branch routes and also main lines had to be content with difficult gradients on grounds of economy, particularly as these lines were often a collection of separately promoted and cheaply engineered projects only later having greater strategic importance.

Being at both ends of the railway construction period, it is of some interest to compare the gradients on the London & Birmingham and Great Central Railways and to find that both were finely engineered.

Apart from the steep incline from Euston to Camden, worked initially by fixed engines, the L&B had to contend with four main summits at Tring, Blisworth, Kilsby and Berkswell. To minimise the limitations of early motive power, Robert Stephenson took great care in the selection of the route, with the result that the bulk of the line was built with gradients of 1 in 330 or less, although this was only achieved with some notoriously difficult engineering. Similarly, the maximum gradient permitted on the London extension of the Great Central was 1 in 176 in order '. . . to secure a first-class running line, as direct as possible, and with easy curves and flat gradients, so as to admit of high speeds'.

Most famous of all inclines in the area was, of course, the Lickey, which raised the Midland's Gloucester to Birmingham main line into the Lickey Hills. Other notable locations where locomotives could be seen hard at work, are portrayed in this chapter.

Left: Sharnbrook: Coal train workings from the Midland collieries to London and the South-East formed a large proportion of the southbound heavy freight on the Midland main line and to minimise the gradients for these trains, the slow lines at Sharnbrook were built with an easier grade but with heavier earthworks and more tunnelling than the original tracks now forming the fast lines. Class 4F No 43888 begins the descent of Sharnbrook bank in September 1961. The fast lines are just out of the picture on the right hand side.   *M. Mensing*

Below: Sapperton: Splendidly turned out, Castle class 4-6-0 No 5083 *Bath Abbey* climbs out of the Golden Valley at Sapperton on a Gloucester to Paddington express in the late 1950s.   *R. E. Toop*

Above: Harbury: Class 8F 2-8-0 No 48449 climbs through Harbury cutting between Leamington and Banbury with a coal train off the former LNW line through Kenilworth and Warwick in September 1956. *M. Mensing*

Below: Leighton Buzzard: A heavy stone train hauled by another 8F, banked at the rear, struggles up the steep grade into Leighton Buzzard from the LNW's Dunstable branch in the early 1960s. LNW 0-8-0s could be regularly seen on this branch until virtually the end of steam, assisting with the working of these trains. *Brian Parnell*

10 Railway Structures

Railways are not merely two rails a fixed distance apart, they relate to the environment and one is an influence on the other. Undulating country requires cuttings and embankments, valleys viaducts, and hills tunnels. Even when a track bed has been formed a whole range of facilities have to be provided before trains can run. Civil, signal and mechanical engineering are all called into play to provide the appropriate specialised equipment.

When railways were first constructed, engineers were at the boundary of known technology and the public's fears, raised by some commentators, had to be allayed. It was, for example, confidently predicted that runaway trains would reach 120 mph after descending the incline through Box Tunnel or that massive rockfalls would block the tunnel. It is a measure of the

greatness of such men as Brunel and Stephenson that the structures they designed still carry trains today, particularly with the elementary techniques available to them. It also points to a theme of Victorian engineering, overdesign for contemporary requirements. This reached its ultimate development in the Great Central London Extension, which carved across ridge and vale in a relentless progress towards its objective.

However, it is in the trackside furniture that the individual character of each line was most apparent. In short, in the railway scene the whole is greater than the sum of its constituent parts, so that the backdrop reflects the style and atmosphere of the area as well as the company that built it. Some attempt is made here to isolate and describe some typical key parts.

Below: Kineton, on the erstwhile Stratford-upon-Avon & Midland Junction Railway, exemplifies the type of signalbox found at many wayside stations throughout the area. Distinctive features are the LMS Kineton board, extensions to the box at both ends to accommodate electric train staffs and a small platform, added when the station platforms were cut away, for the signalman to exchange tokens with the enginemen.   *Rae Montgomery*

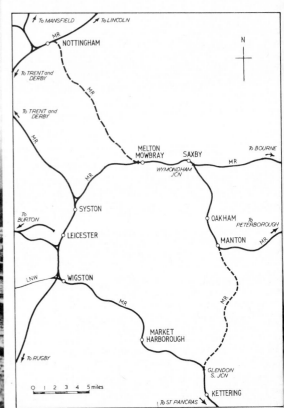

Top left: To service the steam locomotive, one of the essentials is a supply of water. The somewhat unusual water column at Bearley provisioned the Alcester branch engine from the Edstone Aqueduct carrying the Stratford-on-Avon Canal. A leather bag was attached to the pipe for insertion in the locomotive tank, and a wheel valve controlled the flow of water. To water, locomotives had to go beyond the controlling home signal seen in the background.   *Rae Montgomery*

Above: This bridge over the Stratford-upon-Avon & Midland Junction Railway carried the Stratford & Moreton Tramway. Opened in 1826, it was a project of William James, who envisaged it as the first stage of a tramway from Stratford to London. Ultimately it fell into the Great Western net, who converted the section from Moreton-in-Marsh to Shipston on Stour into a conventional branch, while the unconverted section northwards to Stratford declined and eventually closed in 1926.   *M. Mensing*

Far left: As part of the plan for the first 100 mile non-stop runs on the Great Western, water-troughs were laid at Basildon between Pangbourne and Goring and the locomotive tenders fitted with the necessary scoops. Here a Dean 4-4-0 collects water, reputedly the first up train to use them, in 1895.   *A. C. E. Notley Collection*

In order to afford some relief to its main line, the Midland promoted two cut off lines (*left*), one of which ran from Glendon South Junction to Manton. To cross the wide valley of the Welland, the Welland or Harringworth Viaduct (*below*), 1,275yd long and 60ft high at its maximum, was necessary. Closure to regular passenger traffic in 1967 means that only freight trains now cross the valley.   *Andrew T. David Collection*

Box Tunnel, 3,212yd long, was built on a gradient
of 1 in 100, dead straight and falling towards its western
end. To reassure the fainthearted the tunnel mouths were
much larger and more ornate than necessary, apparent in
an 1883 view of the west portal. Brunel, by skilful
surveying, ensured that the sun's rays would penetrate the
tunnel on his birthday, 9 April, to provide an annual
memorial for the group that gathers at sunrise.
British Rail, Western Region

11 Signals and Signalling

One of the distinguishing characteristics of the pre-grouping railway companies was their signalling practice. Each company had its own type of box and signals, either manufactured by the company itself or purchased from a signalling contractor. Particularly noticeable was the angle of the arm when clear or off, ranging from a bare sag of 20 degrees on the LNW, through the 60 degrees of the Great Western, to the near 90 degrees of the Great Northern.

At one extreme stood the Great Western which manufactured and maintained virtually everything, even down to clocks, at its Reading signal works. It standardised on lever frames of its own design and was lavish in its provision of shunting and distant signals. By contrast the Great Central and Great Northern purchased their equipment. On its London extension the former used exclusively Railway Signal Company equipment while the latter used many manufacturers, but principally Saxbys. The GC extension boxes had spare levers for future developments and some opened with more levers spare than working.

As befitted the Premier Line, LNW signalling was elephantine and its signal frames were far more massively built than any other. While it provided shunt signals less extensively than others, it provided distants in profusion, mainly working and not fixed. In an echo of its locomotive practice, the Midland believed in many small boxes, with the locking equipment above floor level.

Standardisation began in grouping days, particularly under A. F. Bound on the LMS, and was continued by BR. Today's multiple-aspect colour-light signalling, although technically more advanced, lacks the visual appeal of the semaphore.

Alleging the Great Central viaduct interfered with signal sighting, the LNW erected, at GC expense, a massive gantry, known as the Rugby Bedstead. Every lower level signal was repeated on the upper to give 44 arms on the second largest signal gantry in the British Isles. When the LMS removed it, it provided enough sections for gantries at Rochdale West, Beeston South, Newbold and Brewery Sidings, Manchester.

Radio Times Hulton Picture Library

Above: Great Western signalling practice is apparent at Bearley East Junction Signal Box where the single track curve to Tyseley and Alcester was worked by tablet instruments, later key token, as far as Bearley North Junction. The speed restriction board indicates a maximum of 25 mph through the junction to Stratford, while the curve was limited to 5 mph. On the bracket signal, the arms indicate the priority afforded to the main line and the distant arm for Bearley North is fixed.

Rae Montgomery

Left: A reminder of the pre-grouping era remained at Reading as late as 1936 in the signals at the up end of the down main line platform, where one arm was lettered 'To SE&C'. Two of the posts also support the down main signals for the Bristol and West of England routes. In the distance, amid the forest of semaphores, is Reading Main Line East Box.

Rev A. W. V. Mace

Above: On the Culworth Junction to Banbury line, Eydon Road Cabin stands virtually completed, typical of the style of GC London extension for which the Railway Signal Co was the signalling contractor. The two stop signals are pitch-pine stone coloured posts with cedar arms, capped by ball and spike finials, supported in each case by guy posts on the other side of the line. *Leicestershire Museums, Art Galleries and Records Service*

Below: The Great Northern employed somersault signals, so called because of the motion of the arm when it fell to clear, as seen at Peterborough. In the foreground are levers, weighted to return to normal, for hand operation of the yard points, while beyond the bridge is the 60 lever Westwood Junction box. Beyond that is the Midland gantry allowing movements from the Midland and M&GN lines to the GN by a crossover immediately behind the bridge piers. *Radio Times Hulton Picture Library*

Despite later additions, notably a track circuit diamond sign and two corrugated steel distant arms, a strong Midland atmosphere remains at the down end of Desborough & Rothwell station in 1966. Midland signalling practice is evident in the style of the gantry, cranks, weights and finials, while the spectacle plate is restricted on the distant signals and the stop signal is made of wood.

M. Mensing

12 Locomotives

With such a diversity of railway companies, operating methods, type of service and other related factors within the period encompassed by this volume, practically every type of motive power from the smallest tank engine to the largest express locomotive could be found on one line or the other. This chapter and the next portrays just a few aspects of the locomotive scene, a subject which could justifiably fill a separate book.

Motive power developed by the main line companies and BR after nationalisation, with a few notable exceptions, was in no way unique to the area, the various classes being generally widely seen in other parts of the United Kingdom. Yet, the special needs of main line and rural branch in the area may well have played some part in the influence of locomotive design and practice found elsewhere. Examples which come to mind are Collett's 14XX and 61XX classes for rural Cotswold branches and GW London suburban services into the Chilterns, Ivatt's Class 2 2-6-2Ts which in later years could be seen widely on LMR branches in the area, and Class N2 0-6-2Ts which worked into the Northern Heights and Chiltern foothills. Many classes of named main line and mixed traffic locomotive on express and semi-fast workings produced a rich variety of locomotives; 0-6-0, 2-8-0 and 2-10-0 freight locomotive types, in addition to mixed traffic and express engines, ferried goods to and from the busy London marshalling yards on the one hand, while on the other the country branch, with one engine in steam, saw mixed trains of goods and passengers. Such workings have been illustrated in the preceding chapters.

Locomotives from other areas could be seen often at work on foreign lines and a day spent at a busy provincial junction station could produce great variety. In addition, the locomotive exchanges brought new types to lines of the area.

Grouping, nationalisation, the progression from steam to diesel, with the closure of many branch and secondary routes, sadly meant rationalisation and loss of locomotive types. Yet even into the 1960s the WR maintained an air of independence with the development of diesel hydraulics while the mainstay of Midland and Euston line expresses were Peak class and English Electric Type 4s. The Prototype *Deltic* resulted in 22 3,300 hp locomotives to haul principal ER main line services, while a range of less powerful diesel locomotives and shunters were introduced for semi-fast, suburban, goods and shunting duties.

While electrification and dieselisation have brought operational efficiency and greater speed, many railway lovers must surely still occasionally hanker for the combination of steam and hot oil which brought so much pleasure to past generations.

Collett 14XX Class 0-4-2T No 1424 is captured at speed as it approaches Standish Junction with the 15.09 Gloucester to Chalford motor train in July 1963.
D. H. Ballantyne

Top left: Of interest because of its origins, former Somerset & Dorset Joint Railway tank 0-4-4T No 1230 hides in the depths of the roundhouse at Wellingborough shed in 1933.   *H. C. Casserley*

Left: Resplendent in broad gauge majesty, 4-2-2 *Great Western* exemplifies the stubborn resistance of the Great Western. Having lost the gauge war in 1846, the GW was forced to convert, first to mixed gauge to allow through workings by other companies' trains without break of gauge and finally to abandon, reluctantly, 7ft 0$\frac{1}{4}$in gauge altogether in 1892.
Radio Times Hulton Picture Library

Above: Stanier Class 5 4-6-0 No 44777, piloting a Jubilee 4-6-0, emerges at speed from the south end of Elstree Tunnel into the dappled evening sunshine on a summer's day in 1953.
Locomotive Publishing Co by courtesy of Ian Allan Ltd

Above: GC 4-4-0 No 852 makes a fine study outside the locomotive shed at Woodford Halse in the early years of the century.

Leicester Museums, Art Galleries and Records Service

Top right: The Duke of Buckingham's railway: Steam and diesel era motive power waits in Buckingham, the crossing point during the experimental period when a railbus service operated between Banbury (Merton Street) and Buckingham in the late 1950s.

Sketch by Fraser Cameron

Right: This Aveling & Porter geared locomotive, which spent from 1872 to 1894 on the Brill Tramway, was later sold to Nether Heyford brickworks in Northamptonshire. It was rescued by enthusiasts in 1951 and restored at Neasden LT works. Initially exhibited at the Museum of British Transport, Clapham, it is now at the London Transport Museum, Syon Park.

London Transport Executive

13 Locomotive Facilities

In the steam age, the Mecca of every railway enthusiast must surely have been the locomotive shed. Shrouded in a sooty haze, smoking giants could be found both inside gloomy buildings or lined up outside the yard for their next duty.

This area had a good selection of depots from which to choose. Outside London, several top link sheds could be found with main line locomotives in abundance. New England in Peterborough was an example on the GN, Rugby on the LNW and Oxford, Swindon, Gloucester and Worcester on the GW. Examples of important mixed traffic depots were Hitchin, Bletchley, Northampton, Banbury, Reading and Didcot. A third category was the small depot housing locomotives working local and suburban passenger and branch goods trains, such as Hatfield, Watford, St Albans, Bedford, Slough and Stratford-upon-Avon. A final category were the branch line sub-sheds, often only big enough to house the one or two engines working a branch, and examples were Leighton Buzzard, Aylesbury, Fairford, Tetbury and Tewkesbury.

Many associated facilities could be seen which were essential to the operation of the locomotive. The larger facilities often varied quite considerably depending upon the size of the depot and company practice. A few modern concrete coaling towers could be found but mostly the coaling stage predominated. Water columns,

towers and softening plants were always provided, while ashpits, with hot cinders, were a feature of the yard. Another part of the scene was the turntable, occasionally in the roundhouse, such as Swindon or Spital Bridge, Peterborough, but usually somewhere outside in the yard.

With the demise of steam, by the mid-1960s most traditional sheds had been swept away, replaced by a small number of modern diesel depots sited at strategic points. With the need for regular coaling and watering gone, a daily visit to the shed was no longer necessary so locomotives could be left in sidings at or near signing-on points away from the locomotive shed. Thus a revolution in locomotive operation was achieved in a single decade.

No account would be complete without a mention of the extensive workshops to which all locomotives were sent periodically for major overhaul. Swindon was the hub of GW locomotive construction and repair, while Wolverton had been a locomotive works up to the 1860s. Further facilities were the locomotive testing stations at Swindon and Rugby which enabled new designs and experimental features to be evaluated.

Now most of this atmosphere has gone and only the preservation society can provide something of the unique flavour of the locomotive running shed.

Top left: Built in 1877, Midland 4-4-0 No 311 stands outside the impressive roundhouse at Spital Bridge, Peterborough, an LMS enclave in LNE territory which supplied motive power to the former Midland lines and after 1932 LNW lines to the west of Peterborough through Stamford and Wansford. *H. C. Casserley*

Left: The fascination of the shed is apparent in this view of part of New England, Peterborough, on a beautiful June day in 1957. Spotless Class A2 Pacific No 60514 *Chamossaire* receives attention next to mixed traffic Class K1 2-6-0 No 62014 and austerity WD 2-8-0 No 90165. *British Rail, Eastern Region*

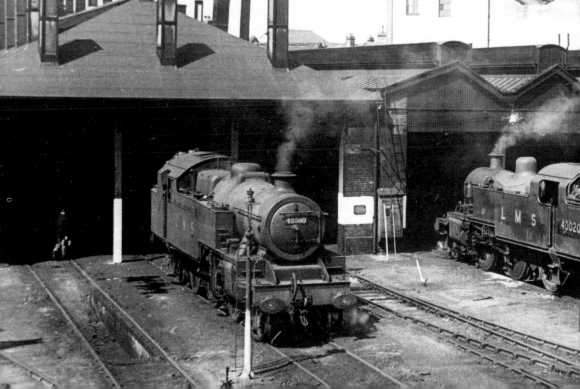

Above: Nearby in the Vale of Evesham, Tewkesbury contrasts in its simplicity. Lurking in the single road shed, Midland Class 3F 0-6-0 No 43754 stands dead as Saltley Class 4 2-6-0 No 43046 is coaled at the coaling stage. Tewkesbury, on the Midland branch from Ashchurch to Great Malvern, remains a quiet rural town on the edge of the Vale of Evesham. *G. D. Braithwaite*

Top left: Gloucester (Horton Road) was an important GW shed on the fringe of the Cotswolds. Of particular interest is the difference in design of the sheds, each road of which was gated at its entrance. In the yard, 5101 class 2-6-2T No 4141 is replenishing its water, while 5205 class 2-8-0T No 5218 stands by the turntable. *Rev A. W. V. Mace*

Left: Still with 'LMS' on their tanks, Fowler Class 3 2-6-2Ts Nos 40010 and 40020 – the regular St Albans and Stanmore branch engines – and Stanier Class 4 2-6-4T No 42590 stand outside the former LNW shed at Watford Junction in April 1949. Built chiefly to house locomotives to work London suburban and branch passenger and goods services, the cramped shed, in the triangle at the junction of the main line and St Albans branch, could only be reached by awkward manoeuvring using the turntable. The site was later used for a car park after electrification of the main line. *H. C. Casserley*

Above: The tranquil setting of the former station and branch engine shed at Tetbury has all the characteristics of the classical GW branch terminal. Being a shed with a simple but rather unusual design incorporating the water tower, the whole location presents the ideal for the modeller. *H. C. Casserley*

Top right: Just outshopped from the works at Swindon, an ex GW 43XX class mixed traffic 2-6-0 and a heavy freight 28XX class 2-8-0 are ready to return to traffic. Running-in turns often produced spotless Kings and Castles on local stopping services between Swindon and Bristol or Didcot as well as locomotives such as these. Although no longer the key locomotive, carriage and wagon works it was, Swindon still plays an important role in diesel unit maintenance. *R. E. Toop*

Right: Once a common scene, but now seeming very primitive, Midland 0-6-0 goods engine No 23011 is manually coaled at the stage at Kettering. Such facilities were supplied with coal from wagons as shown in the picture. *H. C. Casserley*

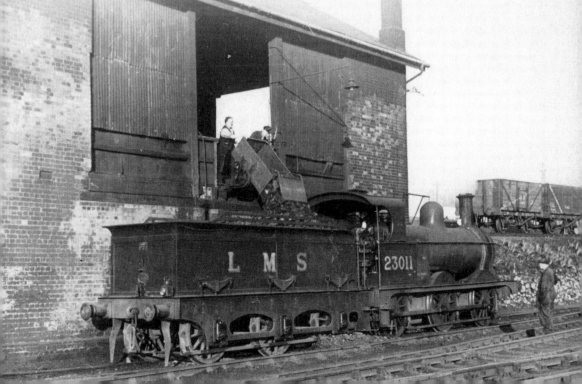

14 Stations

Stations are far more than places to join trains. Shop window, factory floor, showroom, restaurant, a place to meet, to wait and to leave, all of these and more are the functions of a station. Added to this is the varying range of importance from that of a mere wayside halt to that of a main line terminus and, since this is where the railway meets its public, each company felt it incumbent to strike the right note of dignity and individuality.

Consequently a heterogeneous selection of stations could be found in many architectural styles. The earliest lines essayed in a Regency or Classical style, which found a late echo in Bath Green Park of 1870, but turned to Italianate of which Reading and, to a lesser extent, Buckingham are good examples. Apeing the Woburn estate buildings, the Bedford Railway adopted *cottage orné*, most notably at Fenny Stratford. Stamford East and Cirencester Town exemplified the Tudor style while the Northampton and Peterborough line stations are fine examples of Jacobean and Elizabethan.

Station standardisation begins to appear in the Leicester & Hitchin extension of the Midland and finally flowers into the visual unity of the Great Central London extension. Edwardian elegance and drive characterises High Wycombe while Welwyn Garden City portrays the 1920s style and Luton the 1930s. Building materials ranged from the wood of Oxford to the stone of Bath but were most commonly brick, frequently carried by rail, particularly Flettons by the GN from Peterborough. Iron and glass usually formed platform awnings as at Wellingborough and Kettering.

With such a variety of styles and materials sympathetic renovation can thus ensure that some of yesterday's stations can serve and adorn the railway of today.

Below The original 'Marlow Donkey', 0-4-2 saddle tank 522, which lasted until 1935, stands at Marlow around 1880. Principally promoted by Marlow businessmen, including Wethereds the brewers, the Great Marlow Railway from Bourne End was opened in 1873. When it was absorbed into the GW in 1897, a possible extension to Henley was mooted for which the station layout would have required little alteration.
British Rail, Western Region

Wotton in Buckinghamshire had two stations vying to cater for its needs. The first to be built was on the Duke of Buckingham's Wotton Tramway, a private railway opened to passengers in 1872, whose complex history ended in 1935 with London Transport operation. It was a wooden platform (*above*) on a single track with two sidings for freight traffic and was one of the three staffed stations on the line. *London Transport Executive*

The second (*below*) was on the GC line from Grendon Underwood to Ashendon Junction. In common with many of the stations on this alternative GC approach to London, using the GW&GC Joint rather than the Met&GC Joint, the platforms were served by loops off the main line and fairly extensive goods facilities were provided. At its opening on 20 November 1905, it came under the control of the stationmaster of the Tramway station. *D. Thompson*

These views show how the Great Western used stone in its passage through Bath. Buil on a curved site, the mixed Tudor and Italianate style station buildings originally adjoined an overall roof spanning four tracks. Subsequent reconstruction produced a three-track layout and an up bay. To provide good visibility, the signalbox was raised above the platform awnings. *Left* is a recent view showing a diesel-hauled express leaving for London; *below*, a 1921 view of the four-track layout; and, *right*, a detail close up of the stone buildings.
Bath Reference Library;
L & GRP; G. F. Heiro

Right: Hatfield exemplified standard Great Northern building, although with the addition of a private waiting room for the Marquess of Salisbury who lived at Hatfield House nearby. Peculiarities were the staggered platforms, not provided for the up fast, and a parcels platform separated by a ramp from the main up platform. Subsequent alterations including rebuilding in the 1970s have changed the station greatly from this view of about 1875–80. *British Rail, Eastern Region*

Left: Chipping Norton Junction, renamed Kingham in 1909, was at the point where the branches from Banbury and Cheltenham met the Oxford and Worcester main line. The *Langston Arms*, the stone building to the left, had an entrance from the station footbridge and together with the station was intended to form a focal point for this part of rural Oxfordshire, a design which never reached fulfilment. *British Rail, Western Region*

Above: In 1935, the GW station at Banbury still retained its overall roof of 1850 but with only two through lines it became an intolerable bottleneck. To rectify this, and to enable connection to be made with the adjoining LNW branch to Verney Junction, a new station with four through lines was opened in 1958. Ideally suited to the operating requirements of the 1950s, the changed pattern of service since then has rendered it too large for today's needs. *British Rail, Western Region*

Top right: Alcester would have been an undistinguished stopping place on the Midland route from Barnt Green to Cheltenham via Evesham were it not for the presence of a Great Western service from Bearley. To mark this, the station originally had separate booking halls for Midland and Great Western passengers and the GW had its own one-road engine shed at the junction. *W. J. Adcock, MBE, MPS Collection*

Bottom right: The V-shaped nameboard and elaborate signal finials proclaim Midland ownership at Luffenham. The main buildings, built of stone, lie to the left and beyond them is the goods yard. An LNW train from Stamford for the Seaton line stands in the platforms and will diverge from the Midland line to Oakham at the junction just beyond the level crossing from where the picture is taken. *Rutland County Museum*

Above: Northampton's original station was a good example of John Livock's work on the Northampton & Peterborough Railway. In an Elizabethan style, it had two gables separated by stone balustrades and was set off by a simple platform awning supported by scrolly brackets. However, Castle became the main station after its opening in 1882 and Bridge Street, as this station was named, finally saw its last passenger trains in 1964.

Locomotive & General Railway Photographs

15 Railwayana

The influence of the railway can be seen in tangible form beyond the boundary fence. Many a town, like Abingdon, has a Railway Inn in Station Yard, names which linger on after the railway has gone. Indeed, 40 years on, Brill still has Tramhill and a Brill Station postbox, while the Great Northern Inn in St Albans commemorates that company's erstwhile service to the town. Bromsgrove graveyard contains the graves of two men killed by a locomotive boiler explosion while two 60ft diameter tunnel ventilation shafts break surface at Kilsby. Each company's obsession with placing its name or initials on everything it owned could produce cottages at Blisworth inscribed 'SMJR 1914' or spandrels inscribed 'B & C', Bedford & Cambridge, at Sandy. Of course cast iron notices could be found in profusion, culminating at Aylesbury

with a joint injunction by the 'Great Western & Great Central Railways Joint Committee' and the 'Metropolitan & Great Central Joint Committee'.

Similarly, the railway produced ephemera in profusion. Apart from handbills advertising the facilities provided, certain companies issued official postcards, sometimes in colour, of views of their system or places nearby. As collector's items they have been joined by the railway ticket, since nowadays the Edmondson card is becoming increasingly scarce, those issued in pre-grouping days particularly so. Reproduction posters now adorn many a collector's wall while station signs, maps, railway clocks and locomotive nameplates are prize possessions. Together with oil lamps, platform barrows, cattle docks and stables they find no place in today's railway.

Below: To mark the boundary of its property, the Great Western Railway erected a distinctive type of mushroom cast-iron post, about 1ft high and 1ft in diameter. This example is at Kingham where the former Chipping Norton line is crossed by a roadbridge.   *B. Davies*

Right: Between Potters Bar and Brookmans Park on the up side of the GN main line stands a stone obelisk, carrying the City of London arms, erected to facilitate administration of the dues on coal and wine entering London. Dating back to 1694, they were codified by an Act of 1861 and the dues on all such goods passing these posts were, until their abolition in 1889, payable to the City Corporation and used for construction and improvement works. A similar obelisk stands on the down side of the main line from Euston between Hatch End and Carpenders Park.

R. Davies

Left: William Whitbread played a prominent part in the railway development of Bedfordshire and spurred the Midland Railway into constructing the Leicester & Hitchin extension. In Southill Park, where parties picnicked on the Leicester & Hitchin opening day, a monument was erected reading 'To William Henry Whitbread, Esquire for his zeal and energy in promoting railways through the County of Bedford 1864 Erected by Public Subscription'.

R. Davies

Right: Between April and September 1838, road coaches were provided between Denbigh Hall, north of Bletchley, and Rugby for through passengers on the London & Birmingham Railway, since Kilsby Tunnel had not been completed. Time has seen the demolition of the Denbigh Hall Inn, where the change took place, as well as Denbigh Hall signalbox, leaving only an inscription on the A5 roadbridge as a tangible reminder of those early days. *R. Davies*

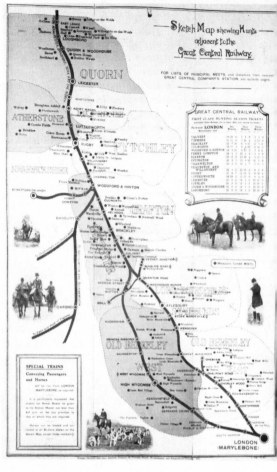

Above left: The ramshackle nature of the Oxford, Worcester & Wolverhampton meant that little heed was paid to the clock but one of its timepieces still graced its former offices at Worcester (Shrub Hill) in 1962.

E. H. Sargeant

Above right: To attract traffic, the Great Central established a publicity department in 1902. Capitalising on the country through which its London extension ran, special Hunting Arrangements leaflets were produced, which for the 1908–9 season, had a map of the hunts, tickets, trains, and special facilities.

Leicestershire Museums, Art Galleries and Records

Service

Below: Closure of Adlestrop in 1966 did not mark the end as one of the station nameboards was removed to the village. In its shelter, weary travellers can rest on a former platform seat and hear the song of 'all the birds of Oxfordshire and Gloucestershire'.

R. Davies

16 Modernisation

In a sense modernisation is a continuous process as the railway scene is never static. Yet the 1950s, and particularly the 1960s, changed the whole face of the railway system.

The 1955 Plan for the 'Modernisation and Re-equipment of British Railways' envisaged the expenditure of £1,200 million over a 15 year period and was expected to attract a return of £85 million a year. The infrastructure was to be modernised, steam was to be replaced by diesel and electric traction, rolling stock was to be replaced, freight services were to be remodelled by fitting continuous brakes to wagons together with resited and modernised yards and terminals; about £35 million was to be spent on 'sundry other items'. In short equipment was to be modernised but attitudes and services were to remain largely unchanged.

By 1960 increasing railway deficits indicated that the plan was not achieving its expected results. The appointment of Dr Richard Beeching ultimately resulted in 'The Reshaping of British Railways' report of 1963. It envisaged the limitation of railways to dense flows of traffic, of types suitable for trainload movement, benefiting from the speed and reliability of railways. It was expected to operate the system to develop these features to the full and 'The Development of the Major Trunk Routes' report of 1965 selected routes for future intensive use.

Implementation of the Beeching Report, especially the contentious closure proposals, left few parts of the railway system unchanged. The motive power, rolling stock, track, structures, signalling and buildings of the railway system of today show considerable changes from 1955.

Below: On 2 February 1959 four lightweight railbuses entered traffic for service between Kemble, Cirencester and Tetbury. Concurrently three additional halts were opened and guards began to issue tickets. Tetbury branch passengers increased by 150 per cent but, because the railbuses were too light to operate track circuits reliably, they could not carry passengers through to Swindon. Ultimately unsuccessful, passenger services were withdrawn from both branches on 6 April 1964.
Colin G. Maggs

Above: Main line dieselisation took a different course on the Western Region than on other parts of BR, where hydraulic transmission was preferred to electric. Subsequent standardisation led to the withdrawal of the hydraulic locomotives after no more than 15 years or so and the last examples were the Western class. One of the class heads a stone train from Westbury to Bletchley through Pangbourne, one of the increasing number of such trains running from quarries to specialised stone handling terminals. *British Rail, Western Region*

Top right: A major project was the electrification of the former LNW main line, together with the Northampton loop, completed in 1966. The subsequent decade has seen considerable expansion of main line services, while stopping services have contributed to growth in housing and population from Hemel Hempstead as far out as Northampton. The marriage of old and new is well illustrated in Tring cutting where trains cut through the Chiltern chalk escarpment. *R. Davie.*

Right: An intermediate stage between existing railway technology and the Advanced Passenger Train is the High Speed Train, seen on trials near Pangbourne in preparation for production orders for passenger service. Formed into units, a 2,500 hp power car is marshalled at each end of seven coaches. Designed for top speeds of up to 125 mph, production units have been built for Bristol and South Wales services and similar units will operate from King's Cross. *British Rail, Western Region*

90

17 Preservation

Echoes of the past are found in all walks of life. Whether the remains of a Roman settlement, an historic cathedral or a relic from the industrial revolution, it is surprising how much has survived to help historians reconstruct something of the life style of previous centuries.

Since World War II, railway rationalisation and modernisation has led to a series of rapid changes, and much of the former railway scene has been swept away forever. To those prepared to seek it, however, much still remains either within the preservation movement, privately or on those few parts of the BR network which have so far escaped modernisation.

The railways themselves provide the basic source of preservation. Here, many of the stations and railway structures are still basically original, although railway closures and the trend towards simpler station buildings has meant the disappearance of many ornate examples. Signal boxes and semaphore signals are still fairly widespread although signalling modernisation through the requirements of higher speeds and economy is causing the rapid replacement of the older style. A few lines, such as Bedford to Bletchley, still retain relics stemming from pregrouping times, but none of these remains have an assured future.

It must therefore fall to preservation societies to save small parts of the railway as working museums, and there are notable examples within the area. Relying on volunteer support and with slender resources, the struggle to maintain relics which often have to be left in the open air, is a time consuming and sometimes thankless task. However, these groups do save valuable pieces from destruction and deterioration and deserve the full support of both the public and enthusiasts.

Much has also been saved privately, but this sometimes means loss of access to the general public. Redundant stations and railway houses have been converted into private dwellings thereby assuring their future. In addition, local authorities are alive to the benefits of converting old trackbeds into bridle ways and nature trails, but such schemes are inevitably limited by finance.

Lack of co-ordination in preservation means lack of progress and if the most valuable remnants of the railway scene are to be saved for the future, there is surely a need for close liaison between the railways, local authorities and preservation socieites to save for future generations some of the railway heritage of the Chilterns & Cotswolds.

Left: The Great Western Society. Symbolic of the ultimate achievements of preservation, a splendid array of former GW motive power is lined up outside the Society owned engine shed at Didcot. This centre not only preserves a former GW locomotive shed, but also provides facilities for maintaining steam locomotives for public runs on BR lines.   *Great Western Society Limited*

Above: An example of the valuable co-operation which can be achieved between BR and preservation societies is the running of special steam trains over BR lines. Most are over main lines as depicted in the frontispiece picture but some are on branch lines. GW Society 0-4-2T No 1466 takes an auto-train along the Wallingford branch on 21 September 1968.
J. G. Mallinson

Quainton Road. Providing a resting place for
former industrial as well as BR locomotives, preservation
societies have rolling stock variety in plenty. Formerly
owned by Associated Portland Cement, 0-4-0ST No 3 is
watered between duties on a Quainton Railway Society
open day. To the left of the water column is 0-6-0PT No
7715, a former GW locomotive obtained from London
Transport who used it on engineers' trains.   *M. D. Grant*

...ene Valley Railway. Centred on Wansford,
...eopening of the line to Peterborough is an integral part of
...e Nene Valley Park. The main locomotive attraction is
...ormer BR Standard Class 5 No 73050 seen here in
...Vansford station about to propel a train to Yarwell
...unction.   *M. D. Grant*

Index